Who Keeps the Water Clean? Ms. Schindler!

written by
JILL D. DUVALL

photographs by
LILI DUVALL

Reading Consultant
LINDA CORNWELL
Learning Resource Consultant
Indiana Department of Education

CHILDREN'S PRESS® *A Division of Grolier Publishing*
New York • London • Hong Kong • Sydney • Danbury, Connecticut

Dedicated to Spencer Schindler

Special thanks to Diane Schindler and her coworkers at Cox Creek

Library of Congress Cataloging-in-Publication Data
Duvall, Jill.
    Who keeps the water clean? Ms. Schindler! / written by Jill D. Duvall ; photographs by Lili Duvall ; reading consultant, Linda Cornwell.
       p.   cm. — (Our neighborhood)
    Summary: Describes the activities of a sewage disposal plant worker who makes sure that the machines are functioning properly to keep the neighborhood's water clean and safe.
    ISBN 0-516-20315-0 (lib. bdg.)—ISBN 0-516-26153-3 (pbk.)
    1. Sewage disposal plants—Juvenile literature. [1. Sewage disposal. 2. Occupations.] I. Duvall, Lili, ill. II. Title. III. Series: Our neighborhood.
    TD743.D89   1997
    628.1—dc20

                                    96-34908
                                           CIP
                                         AC

Photographs ©: Lili Duvall

Ms. Diane Schindler takes care of the equipment at a waste-water treatment plant.

Waste water is water that has been used by the community.

The water must be cleaned at the treatment plant before it can be put into the river.

Ms. Schindler and another worker check the cleaning tanks.

Every day, thirteen million gallons of waste water are sent to the treatment plant. The waste water comes from many neighborhoods.

Some of the equipment
is underground.

Before Ms. Schindler can work, the air must be checked for dangerous gases.

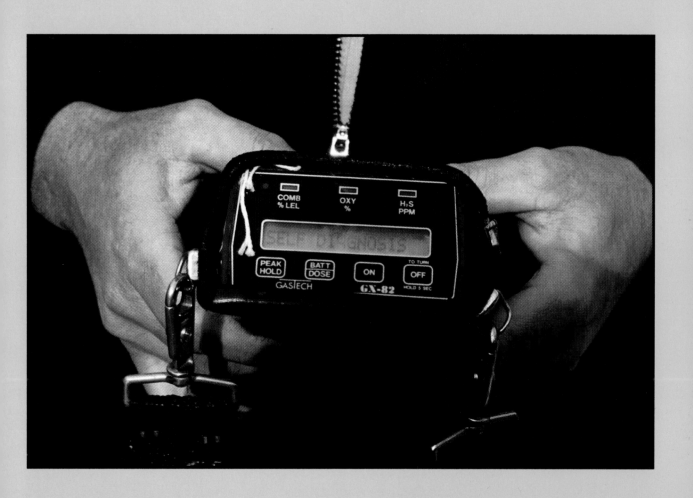

A meter shows that the air is safe.

Ms. Schindler climbs underground.

She checks the equipment. It is working very well!

The air from underground is pushed through a box of wood chips to clean it. This keeps unsafe gases from entering the outside air.

People who live in the neighborhood know their waste water is cleaned safely.

Ms. Schindler must wear safety gear
when she works . . .

. . . boots, goggles, and gloves.

She has just the right tools for each job—grease guns, a drill . . .

. . . and a wrench.

And she always knows where
to find them!

Clean water is important to the community. Ms. Schindler must keep the equipment working well all day and all night.

She checks the equipment . . .

. . . inside and outside.

The treatment plant is very big. Ms. Schindler uses her car radio to talk with other workers.

Sometimes, she drives around the plant in an electric cart.

Ms. Schindler works with many other people who make the water safe.

One worker uses a computer
to see if there are any problems.

In the laboratory, another worker
checks samples of water.

When the water is finally clean, it goes into the river.

Ms. Schindler has a very special reason for keeping the water and air safe.

Her son, Spencer, is two years old. She works hard to make sure he stays healthy!

The neighborhood is happy
to have clean water.
The ducks look happy, too!

31

Meet the Photographer and the Author

Lili Duvall decided when she was in her teens that she wanted to take pictures. She is now a professional photographer and taking pictures of children is her favorite work. Her home and studio are in Maryland.

Jill Duvall, Lili's writing partner, is also her mother. Jill likes living near Washington, D.C., because much of her studying and writing is about the government. Jill feels that writing is very important and even takes her writing to the beach!